TALES OF THE THEOTOKOS

Mary In the Personal, Historical, Scriptural, and Spiritual Realms.

by John C. Wilhelmsson

Chaos To Order Publishing

San Jose, CA

www.c2op.com

ISBN: 0988656345

ISBN-13: 978-0-9886563-4-5

Cover Art:

Our Lady With the Bowed Head.

Vienna, Austria.

Published October 7th, 2013.

The Feast of

Our Lady of the Rosary.

DEDICATION

For my mother Frances Teresa Wilhelmsson. For it was you who gave me physical life and you who, through Baptism, gave me spiritual life. And that first Rosary I found somewhere about the house and began praying I am sure was left there by you.

THE THEOTOKOS

The Council of Ephesus decreed in 431 AD that Mary is the Theotokos. This term literally means "the one who gives birth to God." The term specifically excludes any understanding of Mary as a god. It rather refers to the human being who gave birth to Jesus Christ—to the Blessed Mother.

CONTENTS

PREFACE

The material in this book is composed of four works originally written in an academic setting. The short story "Twin Fates" has been greatly expanded and the historical article "Mary's Role in the Life of the Church" has been significantly edited, while the theological works "The Theotokos in Sacred Scripture" and "Mary Coredemptrix" remain quite close to their original forms.

All of the works as a whole have been edited in order to elucidate the dual themes of the Blessed Mother as both a subjective personal phenomenon and an objective theological figure. In this way it is hoped that, although this book contains four separate works, it still may be read as a whole.

INTRODUCTION

> *Behold, this child is destined for the fall and rise of many in Israel, and to be a sign that will be contradicted (and you yourself a sword will pierce) so that the thoughts of many hearts may be revealed* (Luke 2:34-35).

These words of the Prophet Simeon to Mary point toward the mystery of her participation in the salvific work of her Son. The nature and role of this participation being something that has fascinated, and divided, Christians down through the ages.

Reactions to the Second Vatican Council seem to have created two different camps in the Church today. The conservatives hold that the opening up of the windows of the Church to let in some fresh air has gone too far while liberals hold that the initial reaction to Vatican II was good yet the Church has now taken a step back in its efforts to engage the modern world. All this while we all step back and wonder what effect Pope Francis might now have on the debate.

However, somewhat lost in this essentially political debate are some important truths of the Christian faith that the Second Vatican Council hoped to elucidate. For, as Rocco Buttiglione has pointed out in his fine book Karol Wojtyla: The thought of the Man Who Became Pope John Paul II:

> *One of the goals of the Council was to unify the cause of truth with the cause of human freedom (p. 128).*

Or, as one might say in a more philosophical sense, to unify objective theological truth with subjective human freedom.

Here we learn a great lesson from Mary. For at the Annunciation (Luke 1:26-38) Mary had the human freedom to either participate or not participate in God's plan. Thus the work of redemption could not have moved forward without the "yes" of human freedom!

Our Lady of Guadalupe, both in her warm words to Juan Diego reminding him not to be afraid because of her maternal protection and in her later words to him explaining the role which only he could play, presents the most human and particular understanding of the Blessed Mother.

> *Listen, my youngest and dearest son, know for sure that I have no lack of servants, of messengers, to whom I can give the task of carrying my breath, my word, so that they carry out my will, but it is very necessary that you, personally, go and plead, that my wish, my will, become a reality, be carried out through your intercession.*

We see here a theme, not unfamiliar in the Biblical narrative of the Annunciation as well, that the work of redemption can only be carried out through the free participation of a particular human being who has been called to the task. Thus, the freely uttered "yes" of Juan Diego is also critical to God's plan.

In this book one goes on a journey with Mary from the Personal, to the Historical, to the Scriptural, to the Spiritual. A journey from the messy and subjective realm of human experience to the immaculate and objective realm of theological truth. A journey from human freedom to divine truth. The "liberal" tendency to focus only on human freedom and the "conservative" tendency to focus only on divine truth are the two great errors of our day. Whereas a balanced view of Mary involves, by necessity, an understanding of both. Therefore, my hope is that this book may not only lead to a better understanding of the person and role of Mary, but to a better understanding of the need to ever seek to unify the cause of truth with the cause of human freedom.

.

***

THE PERSONAL

****

TWIN FATES

I still remember clearly that Monday at work some 20 years ago. I would hardly call it a typical Monday. Life had been very difficult for me of late. Waking up in tears many mornings and having this horrible feeling that I had lost some part of me that was central to my existence.

So, on this morning I was searching for answers. I was thinking of a Christian music concert I had attended at South Hills Church a few months earlier. A young woman named Kristy, who was an acquaintance of mine, had greeted me that evening in such a genuine and caring way that it had left a great impression on me. I thought, if a person like Kristy was a part of a church than that church must be doing something right.

So, on this morning I had a dilemma. I knew that I was missing something important in my life and somehow I had the idea that the thing I was missing was good Christian fellowship. Yet I was a Catholic, and Catholics did not just up and decide one Sunday to go to Protestant churches like South Hills. Still, I was considering calling Kathy and Kristy, whom I always thought of together because they were twins, and asking them if perhaps there was a group at their church I might fit into.

However, by the time the afternoon had rolled around the faithful Catholic part of me had vetoed this idea. Sure I had not found much fellowship at my own parish of late, yet it was bound to turn around. God would provide for me in some way and help me to overcome the severe depression and loss of spiritual meaning in my life. Yet I had to stay true to the Catholic faith in letting Him do that.

I recall a scripture which goes something like; "A man may make many plans, yet God chooses the path" (Proverbs 16:9).

That afternoon a customer came into the locksmith shop. He was an older man with a sense of calm about him. I noticed things like that because I had felt no sense of calm about myself around that time. We struck up a conversation after he noticed a copy of The Screwtape Letters by C. S. Lewis in my shirt pocket (It seemed like appropriate reading for a man in my position). This pleasant older man, named Shelby Granger, asked me; "What church do you go to? I told him; "Saint Frances Cabrini." I asked the same question of him and he said, "I am an elder at South Hills Church." Suddenly, I knew that a path had been chosen for me.

A person who has been severely depressed does not often just march off alone to a new church one Sunday. Yet the message of meeting Shelby Granger had been so clear that I felt a certain sense of spiritual strength and confidence. A sense of strength and confidence that had been absent from my life for a long time. I had not bothered to call Kathy and Kristy that week. I had just called the church office and asked them when their singles group met.

So here I was, just before 9:00 a.m., walking into the midst of these three large round buildings which comprised South Hills Church. I found my way into the centre building where the singles group was supposed to meet. I came across a casually dressed young man about my age named Phil. A short time after striking up a conversation with him another young man came along and asked Phil something about who was supposed to be doing the prayer that morning? It seemed that each week before the singles group met some people went upstairs and prayed. When Phil decided that nobody else was going to come, he excused himself in order to go upstairs. Without even thinking twice, I asked if I could join him.

As I walked up the steps, I was really not sure what I was getting into. I could pray the "Our Father" and the "Hail Mary" quite well but somehow I did not think that they were on the agenda. I did not even know if there was an agenda! Still, it all seemed so exciting to just walk into a church one Sunday and go pray with the first person you ran into.

Phil and I found a quiet balcony and he started to pray. I soon found that it was less like a prayer and more like a conversation. Phil was asking God to watch over the meeting that morning and speaking in a very thankful kind of way. Phil also prayed for me and thanked God that I had come that day. I prayed as well yet I do not remember exactly what I said. It seemed the heart mattered more than the head.

As I came downstairs suddenly there were the twins Kathy and Kristy. They were so happy to see me that they both seemed to light up! After we all exchanged warm greetings, they asked me; "What are your plans?" I told them I was going to the singles group but then they told me that I just had to go to the college group with them as well because it was just so great! The people were friendly and the worship was the best. Yet no reason was necessary for me. For I had found my two guardian angels and I intended to stick close by them.

The singles group meeting was an interesting affair. The men were all dressed in suits and the woman were in what looked like their finest dresses. Never before had I seen such a group of well-dressed young people all gathered together in one place. My California casual attire definitely did not fit in. And in many ways, I did not feel like I fit in. Everything seemed just a bit contrived and everyone seemed like they were trying to impress one another just a bit too much. Definitely not my style. I was hoping to find a place where I could be accepted for who I was and not how I dressed. If the day had ended then and there I never would have returned. Yet I had a date with my two guardian angels at the college group and nothing was going to make me miss that.

Kathy and Kristy were both about 5'2" tall with short blond hair and beautiful smiling round sort of faces. Kristy was the more naturally social of the twins while Kathy was the more serious. I had met them through some mutual school friends of theirs I played volleyball with.

In their modest spring dresses they literally did look like two angels. Much of my emotional problems around that time had been caused by a negative relationship with a Catholic young woman who was a schoolmate of theirs. So I was feeling particularly alienated from the opposite sex at that time. Yet Kathy and Kristy were so genuinely kind and sweet that no amount of alienation could overcome them.

I found them in the foyer, and they took me into the large room where the group was to meet. With one on my left and one on my right they took me around and introduced me as their friend. I remember that all of the people were friendly in a down-to-earth sort of a way. This was not a room full of people who were trying to impress one another. This group of people seemed to hold some deeper truth in common. There was a genuine and kind spirit about them. Much like Kristy had shown to me the night of the concert.

The dress of the guys was mostly casual, like me, but the girls had all of these pretty spring dresses on. And as Kathy and Kristy introduced me around the room, I remember how even the most beautiful girl in the prettiest spring dress was as kind to me as the average guy. What a contrast to society these people were! Everyone was kind and supportive of one another. I felt like I had finally found a real Christian community.

My first day at South Hills Church was somewhat like a dream! I had finally found the group of committed Christian young people who I had been searching for. My adventures were hardly over, yet the college group offered me a good place to go where I could practice and strengthen my Christian faith. I had always imagined that that place would be a Catholic group. Yet God had quite clearly led me elsewhere.

I still attended Mass every Sunday during those years at South Hills. Kathy and Kristy left after that first summer for college. We all remained good friends and I visited them both fairly often. Over the years we fell out of touch. Yet even the years cannot take away the magic of that first day at South Hills Church. When my twin guardian angels watched over me.

THREE YEARS LATER

As I walked up to the church, I found myself not feeling quite sure why I was there? It was Ash Wednesday 1993 and I recall saying to myself earlier that day, "It is Ash Wednesday, I should go to Mass." That is the great thing about being a Catholic. You develop habits and habits die hard. The Protestants may have their wonderful heartfelt extemporaneous prayers and the ability to dance circles around the average Catholic in their Bible knowledge, yet sometimes when life has been hard, I'd trade it all for a well learned habit to guide me through the storm.

The storm then had come a few months earlier in the form of being fired from a youth ministry position at the parish where I grew up. Yet in reality it had been much more than just a youth ministry position to me. For it had been my dream to come back to Saint Frances Cabrini and revive the youth program that had meant so much to me as a teenager.

At first, things had gone very well. A group of teens gathered together who were excited about having a youth group. We began having meetings and even got together one Saturday and painted the old Taheny Youth Centre. I gave them all singing lessons, and we would attend Mass together and sing out God's praise so loud that people noticed!

Then one of my superiors seemed to become jealous of our success. She became quite critical of the things I was doing even to the point of asked me not to teach the kids things from the Bible anymore. I considered her request and prayed for guidance.

The next Sunday I was at Mass and one of the readings was from Second Timothy.

> "All Scripture is inspired by God and profitable for teaching, for reproof, for correction, for training in righteousness; so that the man of God may be adequate, equipped for every

good work" (Second Timothy 3:16).

I met with Debra the next Tuesday and told her that I had prayerfully considered her request and received the response of the scripture passage from Second Timothy. And that, therefore, I would not be able stop using the Bible in the youth group meetings. On the following Friday evening I was called into the Religious Education office and fired. To this day it is one of the most heartbreaking things that has ever happened to me.

That evening as I arrived at Holy Family parish, I still felt the sting of that event which had happened three months earlier. I felt betrayed by the people at my home parish and also just really missed my kids. I had wanted to strike back and fight against the injustice of it all, yet I knew that the scandal might damage the faith of the young people I had been working so hard with. So I decided it would be best for them for me to just walk away.

As I entered Holy Family parish that Ash Wednesday, I realized that it was only the second time I had been in a Catholic church since all of these things had happened in late October. I had gone to Midnight Mass on Christmas Eve, mostly out of habit, and I had also tried to find a place to fit in at South Hills. Yet nothing seemed to be working. Even the young lady I had met at school the year before Karen, who I thought was the right one for me, seemed to want to have nothing to do with me.

Still, I was not as low as I had been three years before. Yet I knew that I needed to find a place to have Christian fellowship in my life once again. Yet first of all, I needed to just figure out which denomination of church I wanted to belong to.

Holy Family was crowded that evening. It had a reputation as being the most spiritually lively Catholic parish in town and that night appeared to be no exception. I remember that the people smelled really good. I recalled some scripture about the sweet smelling praises of God's people. The people also seemed quite warm and friendly toward one another.

In the back of my mind, I thought maybe I would see Karen there that night. Perhaps that was part of the reason I had gone? Karen was going back to Church now! I had prayed for her quite a bit during that past year and it finally seemed to be bearing some fruit (in her life at least).

I had started praying the Rosary for Karen about a year earlier. Karen and I had been in a Career Counseling course that past fall semester at West Valley College. A few years earlier I had become quite depressed when my affections for Catholic young lady had been trodden upon. I thought the reason that relationship had gone so badly was that I had not really prayed about it and put things in God's hands. So as soon as I met Karen I thought; "Here is my opportunity to do things right."

My favorite memory of that fall semester with Karen was the day the class visited the Career Centre in order to do research. Karen was interested in perhaps becoming a nun so I decided on that day that I was interested in perhaps becoming a priest. Although many people had told me I should consider that path in life I never really had felt the call. So my sudden interest on this day was purely generated out of a hope to spend some time with Karen.

In retrospect, this may not have been the most wise thing to do for a young man seeking God's blessing upon a romantic endeavor. Yet sometimes love can cloud a young man's judgment.

Although Karen was the kind of idealistic and intelligent young lady who could have made a great nun, she seemed to give up her inclinations toward the religious life after that day. And since mine had never really been authentic from the start suddenly possibilities opened up for us.

Shortly afterwards we began dating. Our first date was to the College Drama Department's production of Through the Looking Glass by Lewis Carroll. Our second date was to a movie entitled "Hook" which was based upon the Peter Pan fairytale. Both of these themes seemed quite appropriate to me because every time I was with Karen I felt like I was living in a fairytale.

Karen was tall and slim with short light brown hair. She had a beautifully structured face with perfect cheek bones and a wonderful shy smile. She never wore makeup because she never had to. She always wore modest old fashion looking long "Granny Dress" and shiny black shoes. The shoes were the only fancy part of her wardrobe. I think she liked them so much because she had been a tap dancer as a girl, and they reminded her of those happier days.

Karen and I spent a good deal of time together that semester, yet I was never quite sure where I stood with her. There was a sense of mystery about her that always drew me in. I could sense that she was struggling with some sort of inner darkness, yet she never seemed to want to share it with me.

Karen had recently become a Catholic through an adult education program called the RCIA. She had quite an authentic faith, however, it was also a new faith and thus without the benefit of all of those wonderful old Catholic habits that help guide people through life's storms.

Shortly after the semester was over Karen moved away and left no forwarding address. I was hurt that she was suddenly just gone and even moreso because she had not even bothered to call and let me know what was going on.

I felt quite heartbroken and lonely that Advent Season. I remember being at Mass and feeling an incredible affinity for the sufferings of Christ. After the New Year we began to gather together to do youth ministry once again. I decided to talk to my friend and colleague Teresa about the situation. She suggested that I might want to consider praying the Rosary.

I decided to pray a Rosary Novena. This is when you pray the Rosary for nine straight days for the same intention. I had prayed this prayer a few years earlier for another friend who seemed to be in spiritual danger and found it to be very intense. Each evening I would start the prayer kneeling down at my bedside yet, by the end of the prayer, I always ended up laying on the floor in tears! Perhaps the incredible intensity of that first Novena was the reason I had not made a further habit of the Rosary at that time.

If that prayer had been intense the next nine days would be just as wondrous. The first day I saw Karen's quite unique orange Ford Capri in the college parking lot. The next day I saw Karen walking from afar off. Then I ran into a friend of Karen's who had been in our class. Each of those first eight days something remarkable happened that was tangibly connected to Karen. And I went from being a heartbroken and lonely young man with little sense of hope to feeling the strength of God's presence in my life once again. And it was all because of the Rosary!

I was so amazed at all of the things that had happened those first eight days that by the final day I had no idea of what to expect. However, I did know it was going to be a busy day with school early in the morning, work all day, and then ministry in the evening. So I decided to pray the final Rosary of the Novena for Karen early in the morning before I left for school.

My exact intention in that Novena had been that I might see Karen once again so I could give her a book that had been very helpful to me in my faith some years earlier. It was entitled How To Be A Christian Without Being Religious and was by Fritz Ridenour. I could sense that Karen's actions had not been directed at me but were about some deeper spiritual trauma she was going through. And I wanted to do whatever I could to help.

The route I needed to take to West Valley College that morning was somewhat different than it is today. For today a freeway bypasses it all but, in those days, it was necessary to drive through the little town of Los Gatos, where I worked in the locksmith shop, and take a small country highway from there to the town of Saratoga where West Valley College is located.

This was the route that everybody had to take so it got to be rather busy on weekday mornings. And on this morning, it seemed even a bit more crowded than usual. And as I was passing by Los Gatos and starting down Highway 9 toward Saratoga things were particularly backed up.

After the remarkable events of the past eight days, I guess I was wondering in the back of my mind what might happen on that final day of the Novena? Wondering, and daydreaming a bit. Then out of the corner of my eye I saw a car coming down a driveway on the right. I could have passed this car by before it got to the highway, yet I decided to be nice and stop and let it in.

As it got closer, I looked inside and there was Karen waving and smiling at me! For those past nine days I had been praying that I might see Karen happy again and there she was! She was not in her usual orange Capri so there was no way I could have known it was her before I decided to stop and let the car into traffic. We drove near one another down to school and when we arrived, I gave her the book I had been wanting to give to her. We talked a little bit and reconnected but then both of us had to rush off to class.

Although this was a happy reunion my relationship with Karen continued to be on and off. She still seemed rather troubled whenever I saw her, so I continued to pray those Novenas. Finally, one morning at the college I was walking from the parking lot toward class and I saw a figure laying on the lawn. It sort of looked like Karen so I decided to go take a closer look.

There she was, wearing her usual granny dress, yet she looked so pale and troubled that it had been hard to recognize her. I said "Hello" and asked her how she was doing? What followed was the most interesting and honest conversation we ever had. First, she apologized to me for not being a better friend. Then, she told me that she was going through some personal things and made it pretty clear that, as a result of this, she was not interested in having a boyfriend at the time.

Looking back, I guess I could have reacted by being hurt. Yet she just seemed so troubled to me, and her words seemed so honest that, in a strange way I actually felt closer to her on that day than on perhaps any other! This, ironically, as our relationship was apparently ending.

Later that day after class, I was walking near that same spot and thinking things over. Our conversation had seemed so intimate because in a strange way it had been very much like going to Confession. Strange though because when one normally goes to Confession the Penitent makes the Confession and the Priest gives the Absolution. Yet on that morning Karen had done both!

She had confessed that she was sorry for having not treated me better and then she had, in effect, absolved me from any further responsibility that I might feel toward her. The relationship was now effectively over, and I was free to just forget about her and move on with my life. Yet somehow this freedom was troubling to me.

It was troubling because I had a tendency to look at romantic relationships in a cynical light. This was because they often seemed quite shallow to me. Almost like people were exchangeable parts and if this girl or guy did not work out then one could easily just find another one to fill the spot. However, for me love was something that had to be much more noble and permanent than this.

It also troubled me because Karen was obviously in a bad place in her life and needed some sort of love and support. And I had been taught that real love is about caring for other people even when you have nothing to gain, and, in particular, when the one you love is troubled or in need.

I still see that day contemplating all of these things on the lawn at West Valley College as perhaps being the most pivotal one in my life. Was I going to be one of those kinds of people who looks upon others as exchangeable parts? Or was I going to be someone who cares for other people regardless of any personal advantage that might be gained from it? Part of me said, "You have been set free so go and enjoy your freedom." Yet the other part of me realized that by turning my back on a loved one in need I would not be gaining anything but in fact losing everything. Everything good and courageous in my heart and everything noble and beautiful in my soul. Everything that made me believe that there was something greater in this universe than just myself and my needs.

My old friend Nan had told me that the 54 day Novena was a powerful prayer. So that day I decided that instead of abandoning

Karen I would do quite the opposite. I would commit myself to pray for Karen the most powerful prayer I knew how to pray in the most powerful way that I knew how to pray it. I would not be the kind of person who cuts and runs when things look bad, but the kind of person who turns and runs to the battle!

Of all the miracles that happened during that first Novena for Karen, the spiritual miracle that took place in me on that day was by far the greatest! For a heartbroken and lonely young man had been transformed into someone with enough courage, strength, and hope to decide that he was not going to live life just for himself but for others! And this, without doubt, was the greatest fruit of that first Rosary Novena for Karen.

As I walked up those steps into Holy Family parish that Ash Wednesday evening, I was happy to think about Karen and how my prayers seemed to have borne some fruit in her life. Yet now, ironically, I was the one who needed prayer about getting involved in the church again.

The thing that really struck me as I entered the church itself was the huge picture of Our Lady of Guadalupe near the altar. I had prayed all of those Rosary Novenas for Karen in front of an Our Lady of Guadalupe candle so I had naturally begun to develop a devotion towards her. Thus, it felt quite appropriate to find her image there so prominent on that night.

As the Mass began, I remember feeling very comfortable and at ease. I had always loved the motif of Lent. The whole idea of going through a trial in the desert was something I could very much relate to then. Yet even Christ had been given the blessing of having a great mystical experience before he went out into the desert. If only God would have said to me, "This is my servant in whom I am well pleased" (paraphrasing Matthew 3:17) that would have made all of the difference. Yet, beyond all of my own problems, I was beginning to realize that I was surrounded by a lot of people I actually had a good feeling for. For I could sense something beautiful and genuine in those gathered around me on that evening.

Then, at one point during Mass I looked upon the image of Our Lady of Guadalupe and suddenly felt like I had made contact not just with the image, but with the something greater that the image represents. Then I felt the presence of Our Lady of Guadalupe as an even greater calm in my soul and, quite distinctively, perceived her communicating with me saying:

> *"Thank you, John. Thank you for what your prayers have done for Karen."*

Suddenly, right then and there, all of my hurt and disillusionment disappeared. Next, an incredible sense of Love tangibly flowed into my heart. A certitude then came upon me. Yes! I had been scandalized by some people at my old parish and what had happened to me was wrong. Yet the Truths of the Catholic faith did not rest upon just these few people but upon something much greater.

And if Our Lady of Guadalupe is real than her son Jesus is real! And if Our Lady of Guadalupe is real than the Catholic faith, even with all of its problems and faults, is real! She was the Bona Fide! Her words that evening had broken through my frail subjective existence, and I somehow knew right then and there that I had always been a Catholic and that I always would be a Catholic.

Since that time, even though life is still sometimes hard and certainly not perfect, this knowledge and assurance of my Catholic faith has never left me. That moment so many years ago at Holy Family parish the Blessed Mother had gone from being just some objective theological figure into being a real and tangible part of my subjective human existence.

And because Our Lady of Guadalupe had broken through into my subjective human existence my objective knowledge of theology was now much more real for me. Here we see the proper role of mysticism in the Church. Here we see the great role that the quite warm, human, and particular nature of the Blessed Mother can, and often does, play in bringing people to her Son.

Yet even having said all of this I must acknowledge the role that Kathy and Kristy and being at the South Hills College Group played for me. Never before, or since, have I encountered such a sense of genuine Christian community. So much so that from that time forward that wonderful group of young people at the South Hills College Group became my model for what Christian community can be.

In many ways I have been blessed with twin faiths. And I am grateful for what each one has given to me. In the end I believe that they are both genuine examples of faith in Jesus Christ. Only expressed in different, and perhaps even complimentary, ways.

***

***

***

THE HISTORICAL

****

MARY'S ROLE IN THE LIFE OF THE CHURCH

The early Church did much to improve the position of women in the world. In the Roman Empire females were thought to be of less value than males and abortion and infanticide were common. Thus, female babies were often victims of these horrific practices. "The Didache" is a first century document used to train new converts to the Christian faith. It is quite explicit about the prohibition of both abortion and infanticide for Christians.

> …you shall not murder a child by abortion nor kill that which is born.1

The early Christians were so effective at preventing these cruel practices that, within a short period of time, there were a greater number of female than male children in the general population.

Many of these women chose to dedicate their lives to God as celibates. Out of practical considerations they soon began to gather together into communities of Christian nuns. As Owen Chadwick points out in A History of Christianity this was another positive step forward for women.

> As women gathered into communities, some of them learned to read and write, for a community needed members who could read the Bible to them and could talk about it.2

In these early communities of nuns women could often come and go as they pleased and even choose to leave the community all together in order to marry. They were a great step forward for women in general and places of safely, stability, and education.

Later, men followed in this same lifestyle and began the first communities of Christian monks. As the Roman Empire went into decline these communities became more and more popular. Not only as spiritual retreats but also as safe and organized societies. Finally, in 476 AD the Western Roman Empire collapsed. The history of this area then fell somewhat silent until the Middle Ages. Yet in this silence these monastic communities of both women and men continued on.

These groups were at first mostly dedicated to prayer but soon realized the need for educated members who could serve as spiritual guides for the rest of the community. Thus the monasteries, especially after the fall of the Roman Empire, developed into centres of learning. Perhaps the most important reason for this was the function that many of these communities took up of copying by hand the Holy Scriptures and other important writings of the Church Fathers.

With society in decay and the civil authorities in disarray this activity was expanded to include the copying of all writings that were considered to be of cultural value. In this way, these monastic communities served as a sort of seed of knowledge for the later European societies of the Middle Ages to draw upon.

Devotion to the Blessed Mother was no doubt a very important and even central element in the lives of these communities. For the nuns, Mary and her virtues were the model for their entire way of life. Humility, obedience, virginity, and charity were central in the lives of the monks as well. The Blessed Mother was perhaps even more important for the monks because she offered a connection to the feminine in their all male communities.

We can better understand this monastic devotion to Mary by looking at what it eventually developed into. The Middle Age practice of Chivalry being an excellent example of this.

> Chivalry also developed an elaborate code of social conduct along with its military and religious aspects. The social side of chivalry is sometimes called courtesy. It included an ever more complex set of manners, which made the warrior knight into a gentleman capable of proper conduct in court society. The feminine influence seems to have been decisive in the increasing refinement of noble life.3

So here we see within Chivalry a great flowering of feminine influence at the highest levels of society.

The Christian age thus brought with it a far greater value and respect for the lives of women in the form of its strong opposition to abortion and infanticide. This greater respect for women was then preserved and developed in monastic life. And finally, this greater respect for women saw the feminine influence become decisive in the courtly societies of the Middle Ages.

The influence of devotion to the Blessed Mother in all of these areas of improvement for the lives of women should not be underestimated. Yet what can be said of her more direct influence? No look at the role of Mary would be complete without an investigation into the most popular and successful devotional prayer in history—the Rosary.

"Rosary" literally means a closed in rose garden. This seems an obvious allusion to the Garden of Eden. It also leads us back to the monasteries in terms of the great gardens contained within them. These gardens were modeled after the Garden of Eden and often literally brought life to the community.

The Ave Maria prayer itself was taken from the first chapter of The Gospel of Luke with a phrase imploring Mary's intercession added onto the end. The Rosary prayer itself consists of one Our Father and ten Ave Marias which then make up one decade. Different mysteries of the Rosary having to do with the birth, death, and resurrection of Christ later became associated with each decade. The mysteries also each came to be associated later with the particular virtue of Christ, or Mary, which was displayed within it.

Many explanations for the great popularity of the Rosary have been offered. Among them are the physiological good of meditation in general, the focus on the great Christian virtues found within the mysteries, and the feelings of closeness to Christ and Mary that the prayer often elicits.

One important thing to keep in mind with regard to this is that the Rosary was based upon the Holy Office. The Holy Office was prayed by many of the monks and nuns yet generally required more time and education than the usual lay person had. Thus in a sense the Rosary was the prayer of the common person. Most Christians who pray the Rosary would also cite the great power of the prayer to bring about tangible results in real life situations as perhaps being the most important reason for its popularity.

With little doubt the man most associated with the Rosary is St. Dominic. Around the year 1200 AD Dominic was fighting the Albigensian heresy in southern France and the battle was not going well. The Albigensians were a gnostic group that held that the body was evil and the soul was good.

Tradition holds that Dominic, who always visited the churches he was passing by, had an important encounter with the Blessed Mother on one of these occasions.

> On one of these occasions, tradition has decreed that Our Lady appeared to him in the church of Notre Dame de la Dreche. To comfort him in his

> sadness, the Blessed Virgin gave Saint Dominic her especial prayer of the rosary, with the instructions that this prayer should be offered by the people as an antidote to heresy.4

Dominic was quite successful in this effort and the Albigensian heresy was soon put down. His order of the Dominicans later became the great preaching order of the Catholic Church and developed a tradition of knowledge directed by prayer.

The greatest military victory attributed to the Rosary took place in 1571 AD in the Bay of Lepanto. With the Protestant reformation in full swing on the European continent and the forces of Islam in control of the Mediterranean Sea the future existence of the Catholic faith seemed in doubt.

Realizing the serious nature of the crisis Pope Pius V sought to form a "Holy League" to defeat the Ottoman fleet and regain control of the Mediterranean. Yet in order to do so it would be necessary to unite the Doges of Venice with King Philip II of Spain.

However, the Doges of Venice and King Philip II of Spain held no great view of one another because of their own competition over control of the Mediterranean. So, bringing them together would be no small task even for a Pope. Pope Pius V sought to form the alliance based upon the mutual Christian cause of all involved. Yet he also had other tools to use in forging unity.

> The devotion of Pius V to the Blessed Virgin had begun in childhood and her prayer of the rosary was especially dear to him, for the power of prayer over all human vanity was for this man proved beyond doubt. Only two years earlier in a Papal Bull he had instructed the faithful in the prayer of the rosary as the most powerful weapon against error. After he became Pope, he was a

> familiar site in the streets of Rome walking amongst the people clad still in the simple robes of a Dominican monk, deep in the prayer of the Rosary.5

On the feast day of St. Dominic, March 7, Pius V signed his name to the Holy League agreement. He then haggled with the diplomats of Madrid and Venice a full two months before they added their own signatures. That summer the Holy League fleet was assembled in Messina. The Rosary was recited daily on every ship and confessions were heard and mass offered. Finally, the great armada set sail and met the enemy on the morning of October 7, 1571. As foes engaged Don John of Spain, who was in command of the Holy League fleet, spotted the Turkish Admiral's flagship and sailed in to meet it. The Turkish Admiral Ali Pasha was quickly felled by a cannon ball and beheaded. This turned the battle in favor of the Holy

League and by nightfall the Turks had been routed into total disarray.

After this victory, which took place against all odds, Pope Pius V proclaimed October 7th as a feast day in honor of "Our Lady of Victories." Yet it was the Venetians who perhaps gave the most fitting tribute in the form of an inscription on the wall of a chapel built in her honor.

> Neither valour, nor arms, nor leaders but Our Lady of the Rosary gave Victory.6

The Blessed Mother's importance in the life of the Church continues today. Among the miracles modern believers attribute to her are the fall of a communist empire, the miraculous escape from death by an assassin's bullet of Pope John Paul II, and many visions warning of difficult times ahead which can only be avoided through prayer.

References

1. Roberts-Donaldson English translation of the Didache chapter 2. www.earlychristianwritings.com/didache.html

2. Chadwick, 0., (1995). A History of Christianity p. 77. New York: St. Martin's Press.

3. Spellman, F., (Ed.). (1965). The Catholic Encyclopedia for School and Home. First Edition, Volumes 1-12. San Francisco: McGraw Hill Book Company.

4. Vail, A., (1995). The Story of the Rosary. P. 50. London: Harper Collins.

5. Ibid, p. 89.

6. Ibid p. 95

***

***

***

THE SCRIPTURAL

****

Saint John Henry Cardinal Newman

THE THEOTOKOS IN SACRED SCRIPTURE

And this, by the way, may be taken as one remarkable test, or at least characteristic of error, in the various denominations of religion which surround us; none of them embraces the whole Bible, none of them is able to interpret the whole, none of them has a key which will revolve through the entire compass of the wards which lie within. Each has its favorite text, and neglects the rest. None can solve the great secret and utter mystery of its pages. One makes trial, then another: but one and all in turn are foiled. They retire, as the sages of Babylon, and make way for Daniel. The Church Catholic, the true Prophet of God, alone is able to tell the dream and its interpretation.1

John Henry Cardinal Newman's words were written well over a century ago and not only maintain their veracity today but, like a finely aged wine, actually have gained more purity of truth as time has passed. With the expansion of Christian, and pseudo-Christian, denominations spiraling into the tens of thousands many sages continue to come forth, yet the true Prophet continues to tell both the dream and its interpretation.

The one great sign of the controversy among Christian brethren over the interpretation of Sacred Scripture is surprising. For we can all gather around the table and speak of God as Father, Son, and Holy Spirit. And we can all, in one way or another, point to Jesus Christ crucified and speak of our salvation. So Jesus, who was to be the great sign of contradiction to the world (Luke 2:34), ironically is not the greatest sign of contradiction among his followers. For it is rather the mention of his mother Mary's name that often stirs the greatest controversy. She has become to the Church what her son is to the world—a sign of contradiction.

With this in mind let us embark upon our study. With John Henry Cardinal Newman as our guide we shall search for a purely Biblical view of Mary.

Yet first we must begin our journey by coming to a more complete understanding of the role of Christ in the economy of salvation. In chapter five of The Book of Romans Paul speaks of how sin entered the world through the one man, Adam, and thus death came to all. But now the grace of God has overcome death through the one man Jesus Christ. Paul thus sets up the Christ/Adam analogy. He goes on to conclude:

> For just as through the disobedience of one person the many were made sinners, so through the obedience one the many will be made righteous. The

> law entered in so that transgressions might increase but, where sin increased, grace overflowed all the more, so that, as sin reigned in death, grace also might reign through justification for eternal life through Jesus Christ our Lord (Romans 5:19-21).

Later, Paul speaks of how Christ has redeemed not only mankind but all creation.

> We know that all creation is groaning in labor pains even until now; and not only that, but we ourselves, who have the first fruits of the Spirit, we also groan within ourselves as we wait for adoption, the redemption of our bodies (Romans 8:22-23).

So we see an intimate connection here between the fall of mankind and the fall of creation. As in fact both are really the same event brought about by the sin of Adam.

This led Irenaeus of Lyons to speak of the theological principle of recapitulation in Christ.

> When [the Son of God] took flesh and became man, he recapitulated in himself the long history of men, procuring for us the reward of salvation, so that in Christ Jesus we might recover what we had lost in Adam, namely, the image and likeness of God.2

So just as the first man, Adam, had stood in a new creation Christ, the new Adam, has brought about a regeneration of creation. And even though this regeneration in Christ has not been fully realized by all human beings, and bringing about this realization is the very mission and purpose of the Church, it remains a fact. Sin and death have been destroyed and all things have been made new in Christ Jesus!

With this in mind let us begin our investigation into our first passage from Sacred Scripture. In the book of Genesis, a prophetic prediction of salvation is made directly after the story of the Fall. This passage is known as the Proto-Gospel as it serves as the first mention of God's plan of salvation after the Fall. Speaking to the serpent, God says:

> I will put enmity between you and the woman, and between your offspring and hers; He will strike at your head, while you strike at his heel (Genesis 3:15).

So, this first glimpse at the Gospel message shows us that just as one man, Adam, brought about the Fall in partnership with a woman God intends for the recapitulation of creation to take place in a similar manner.

Yet who is this woman whose offspring will crush the serpent's head? Cardinal

Newman in speaking of this passage states:

> In that awful transaction there were three parties concerned, the serpent, the woman, and the man; and at the time of their sentence, an event was announced for the future, in which the three same parties were to meet again, the serpent, the woman, and the man but it was to be a second Adam and a second Eve and the new Eve was to be the mother of the new Adam.3

Having analyzed the passage in general terms he goes on to name the parties involved.

> The Seed of the woman is the Word Incarnate, and the Woman, whose seed or son He is, is His mother Mary. This interpretation, and the parallelism it involves, seem to me undeniable; but at all events (and this is my point) the parallelism is the doctrine of the Fathers, from the earliest times.4

So, Newman, quite strongly, points out that the “Woman” whose seed will crush the Devil's head can only be Mary and has been universally thought to be so since the earliest times.

Irenaeus of Lyons (died 202 AD) had been born in Smyrna and known its Bishop Polycarp who in turn had sat at the feet of the Apostle John and been his direct successor. Thus, he offers a very early and quite explicit understanding of the Proto-Gospel.

> Adam had to be recapitulated in Christ, so that death might be swallowed up in immortality, and Eve [had to be recapitulated] in Mary, so that the Virgin, having become another virgin's advocate, might destroy and abolish one virgin's disobedience by the obedience of another virgin.5

In this understanding our great early theologian, who has already given us the principle of recapitulation, offers us yet another theological principle, namely, recirculation. This in essence means that the process of restoration from the Fall must mirror, in an opposite manner, the Fall itself. Thus, Mary finds her role in the process as the New Eve.

A contemporary of Irenaeus was Tertullian. Tertullian was the first great Latin writer of the Early Fathers. He brings out the principle of recirculation in an even clearer manner.

> God recovered His image and likeness, which the devil had seized, by a rival operation. For into Eve, as yet a virgin, had crept the word which was the framer of death. Equally into a virgin was to be introduced the Word of God which was the builder-up of life; that, what by that sex had gone into perdition, by the same sex might be brought back to salvation.6

Tertullian ascribes an important role to Eve in the Fall. And because of Eve's prominent role in the Fall, when we look at the two events in terms of recirculation, Mary's role in the work of salvation must be seen as being just as prominent.

So, we see emerging in the Fathers, from the earliest times, the Eve and Mary parallel based on their understanding of Genesis 3:15. And the trend continues on, in both the East and West, until the formula becomes so familiar that it is reduced to the simple theological axiom:

Death through Eve, life though Mary.7

We hear this first from Jerome and Augustine in the fourth century and continue to hear it resonant all the way up until the Second Vatican Council in our own day. Thus, Mary replaces Eve as the Mother of Life.

The Early Fathers have often been accused of giving a strictly allegorical interpretation to

Sacred Scripture. On the surface this may seem to be the case in their interpretations of Genesis 3:15 which we have looked at. However, let us examine the question more closely.

The first difficulty encountered when attempting to give an interpretation of Genesis 3:15 is that the literal sense of the passage is difficult to arrive at. This is because Genesis 3:15 is, in and of itself, a prediction of future events. If we, in contrast, look at the Exodus event we can literally say that Moses led the people out of bondage in Egypt; and then build on this by speaking of how their physical bondage was really a sign of a deeper spiritual bondage (allegorical sense), and that spiritual bondage is something each person experiences in their own bondage to sin (tropological sense), and that bondage to sin will finally be completely broken when Jesus comes again and leads us to heavenly glory (anagogical sense).

So, when the Early Fathers are accused of giving strictly an allegorical interpretation to Genesis 3:15 one can fairly ask, if not that what? How does one give a literal interpretation to a prediction of a future event? I would say that the answer depends upon the clarity of the prediction. If the prediction of Genesis 3:15 is, as Newman states, the source of "the great rudimentary teaching of Antiquity from its earliest date concerning her [Mary]" how can it ever be argued that the Early Fathers believed the passage to be literally referring to anyone but her? 8

This particularly in light of the phrase "strike at his head." If this is understood to refer to killing the serpent then who could the "seed" of the Woman be but Jesus Christ? And who could the Woman be but His mother? For who else can claim final victory over the evil one?

In the case of Genesis 3:15 and the New Eve doctrine it can be said that Newman is simply reflecting an explicit view of the Early Fathers. That he is taking a thought which truly belongs to the Early Fathers and handing it on to us. So with the New Eve doctrine we might call Newman a "theological mediator." However, with our second passage from Sacred Scripture Newman's own thought can be said to be more at the heart of the interpretation we shall examine.

Before giving his interpretation Newman feels compelled to explain the relative silence of Sacred Scripture toward the person of Mary. Newman explains this relative silence as being due to the fact that Mary was still present with the Early Church during the writing of most of Sacred Scripture. He believes that since the care of Mary was entrusted to the Apostle John it will be in his writings that one might expect to see the mystery of the person of Mary more fully revealed. In fact, although Mary is present at almost all the important events mentioned in the Gospels, the last words we hear from her in Sacred Scripture are from the Gospel of John. Fittingly enough those words are "Do whatever he tells you" and are spoken at the wedding at Cana in reference to her Son.

Newman believes the Apocalypse of John to be quite possibly the only book of the Bible to be written after Mary had departed to be with her Son. Given this thought and the Johannine authorship of Revelation, Newman believes, almost apriori, that further revelation about the mystery of Mary's presence in the Early Church will be made in the Apocalypse of John.9

But let us not trip over our own assumptions before we go on. Why is it unlikely that much would have been written about Mary while she was still with the early Church? One can say with great piety that her natural humility might have brought this about, and this may be quite true. However, one does not need to rely on piety to come up with the best explanation. The simple fact is that, just as with the Apostles, as long as a person is still around there is no need to write great volumes on who that person is or what that person said. For one can simply observe the person rather than preserve, in writing, their memory. It is only after a person is gone that we feel a natural need to preserve in some way their memory. Add to this the Early Church's need to combat the Christological heresies that revolved around the person of Mary, and one clearly sees that a great profundity of writings about Mary should occur after she is no longer present with the Church.

With this understanding in mind now let us now begin our investigation into Revelation Chapter 12.

> A great sign appeared in heaven: A woman clothed with the Sun, and the

> Moon under her feet; and on her head a crown of twelve stars. And being with child, she cried travailing in birth, and was in pain to be delivered. And there was seen another sign in heaven; and behold a great red dragon ... And the dragon stood before the woman who was ready to be delivered, that, when she should be delivered, he might devour her son. And she brought forth a man child, who was to rule all nations with an iron rod; and her son was taken up to God and to His throne. And the woman fled into the wilderness (Revelation 12:1-6).

The identification of these three characters must be our first task. It is almost universally accepted that the man-child is Christ. This is, no doubt, because of the man child being "taken up to God and to His throne." The great red dragon's identity is also quite apparent. He serves as the primary adversary of the Woman and the man child and thus is identified as the Devil.

Yet this still leaves us the task of identifying the Woman? Let us consider this question. In Genesis 3:15 we have the last meeting of the Woman, the Man, and the Serpent. In Revelation chapter 12 we have already identified two of those parties and know from the text that the Woman is the mother of the man-child Christ. Genesis 3:15 promises a further battle to occur between the Woman, the Man, and the Serpent in which the Serpent is finally and permanently defeated (which finally does takes place in Revelation 20:10).

Yet even with all of this, as the name of the Woman almost screams out from within us, the great majority of interpretations of this passage claim that the Woman represents only the Church.

Newman actually agrees with the great majority of interpretations of the passage, with one qualification.

> Now I do not deny of course, that, under the image of the Woman, the Church is signified; but what I would maintain is this, that the Holy Apostle would not have spoken of the Church under this particular image, unless there had existed a Blessed Virgin Mary, who was exalted on high, and the object of veneration to all the faithful.10

Newman's argument in essence revolves around the origin of the symbol of the Woman. Why would the Apostle John, or any writer for that matter, choose a particular symbol to convey a message? The answer can only be that the particular symbol chosen resonates with the expected readers. So the question now becomes: Why did the symbol of the Woman resonate so well within the early Church? Newman believes this to be so because of the great veneration which Mary, the mother of Jesus Christ, received in the early Church (Not adoration which is due to God alone but veneration which can be given to an exceptional created being). So the Woman of Revelation 12 refers primarily to the Church. Yet she could not do so unless there existed this great veneration to Mary.

We can speak of what a symbol refers to and what a symbol means in and of itself. The Woman most certainly refers to the Church, yet just as certainly gains all of its veracity of meaning from Mary. Newman now goes on to point out something quite surprising.

> Scripture is not fond of allegories. We have indeed frequent figures there, as when the sacred writers speak of the arm or sword of the Lord; and so too when they speak of Jerusalem or Samaria in the feminine; or of the

> mountains leaping for joy; or of the Church as a bride or as a vine; but they are not much given to dressing up abstract ideas or generalizations in personal attributes. This is the classical rather than the Scriptural style.11

First, the Early Fathers and now Sacred Scripture itself! The myth of allegory has been exposed. But what of the Mary/Eve comparison we have invested so much time in?

Actually, the Mary/Eve comparison is exactly the point. For, properly understood, it is not an allegory but an analogy. The difference between the two is that for an analogy to be good it must be done between two things that are equal, while an allegory has no such constraints. So, comparing a person to a person is a good analogy. Especially if those persons are both woman and are both intimately connected to important events in salvation history. Yet to compare a person, the “Woman”, with something like the Church? One can only say, "Bad analogy."

Finally, Newman goes on to say that the Woman in Revelation 12 can be linked to the Second Eve because of the allusion in the passage to the history of the Fall. This allusion can be seen in the ultimate defeat of the serpent mentioned in Genesis 3:15, and the actual defeat of the Devil spoken of in Revelation 20:10 as a completion of the battle that begins in Revelation 12.

Having offered so much evidence for the Woman of Revelation 12 to be thought of as referring to Mary Newman deals with the question of why this is so important.

> But if all this be so, if it is really the Blessed Virgin whom Scripture represents as clothed with the sun, crowned with the stars of heaven, and with the moon as her footstool, what height of glory may we not attribute to

> her? And what are we to say of those who, through ignorance, run counter to the voice of Scripture, to the testimony of the Fathers, to the traditions of East and West and speak and act contemptuously toward her whom her Lord I delighteth to honour?12

Newman seems to be saying that if people, in the name of Christ, are choosing to ignore, and even degrade, Mary how utterly foolish they are. I do not know whether to laugh or cry!

In conclusion, let us consider the outward appearance of Mary early on in the Gospel narratives. She appears to be a teenage girl in a crisis pregnancy yet she is actually the New Eve who carries within her womb the New Adam. Yet this ordinary looking young woman will, in time, be raised to such heights that she will becomes a sign of contradiction to those who seek to follow her Son.

And why? Because we have been looking only at the outward appearance and not at the inner reality. Let us all resolve to ask forgiveness for our pride and seek the inner reality of the role and person of Mary. Yet let us do this not in vain opinion born out of a hurtful past, but in the words of truth which God has giving to us all in Sacred Scripture.

Notes

1. See E. Przywara, The Heart of Newman. San Francisco: Ignatius Press, 1997, p. 91.

2. See L. Gambero, Mary and the Fathers of the Church. San Francisco: Ignatius Press, 1999, p. 53.

3. See J. Newman, Mary: The Second Eve. Rockford, IL: Tan Books, 1982, p. 2.

4. Ibid.

5. See L. Gambero, Mary and the Fathers of the Church. San Francisco: Ignatius Press, 1999, p. 55.

6. See J. Newman, Mary: The Second Eve. Rockford, IL: Tan Books, 1982, p. 3.

7. See Documents of Vatican II Dogmatic Constitution on the Church. N. 56.

8. See J. Newman, Mary: The Second Eve. Rockford, IL: Tan Books, 1982, p. 2.

9. Ibid. p. 17.

10. Ibid. p. 18.

11. See J. Newman, Mary: The Second Eve. Rockford, IL: Tan Books, 1982, p. 18.

12. See J. Newman, Mary: The Second Eve. Rockford, IL: Tan Books, 1982, p. 19.

***

***

***

THE SPIRITUAL

****

MARY COREDEMPTRIX

In examining Mary's role as Coredemptrix let us first examine the etymology of the term. "Co" comes from the Latin root "cum" which simply means "with." Another example of the Latin root "cum" is found in the English word "compassion." In it we find "cum" joined with the word "passion", which in this sense means "suffering", and thus the term means "with suffering." So we might say that to share in the sufferings of Christ is to have compassion.

In Latin "co" never implies equal, and in English it only implies equal in some secondary connotations. However, the official theological language of the Catholic Church is Latin so any definition of Mary Coredemptrix must be true to the Latin meaning of the term.

"Redemptrix", another Latin term, simply refers to a woman engaged in the work of redemption. The "trix" ending is used in Latin to refer to the feminine role. Thus "coredemptrix" means a woman who shares in the work of redemption. The term is by its very nature an open one and does not in any way imply an exclusive role.

For this reason, let us note that the term "coredemptrix" is one properly applied not only to the Blessed Mother but to any woman who helps in the work of redemption. Thus, my mother who had me baptized is a woman, in an instrumental sense, working together with Christ for my redemption. The same can be said of the sisters and lay women who served as my religious education teachers, and my female friends who have prayed for my well-being. Indeed, any woman who has in any way helped me to know Christ or deepen my relationship with Christ can be legitimately referred to as a coredemptrix.

Thus, in this general sense, the use of the term "coredemptrix" to describe the Blessed

Mother should not be seen as being a case of Marian excess but actually could be understood as a case of Marian minimalism. For the term “coredemptrix” can be applied not only to the Blessed Mother but to any woman who helps in the work of redemption. I would equate it to the disturbing practice of referring to Mary as our "sister in faith." For every woman of faith is a sister but we only have one Blessed Mother.

In its proper theological definition redemption actually has two aspects. Objective redemption refers to the acquisition of redemptive grace, while subjective redemption refers to the distribution of that same redemptive grace. So, when I speak of using the term “coredemptrix” in a general sense I am actually speaking of using it only with regard to subjective redemption. For when my mother had me baptized, she did not help to acquire redemptive grace, for only the sacrificial offering of Christ at Calvary can be said to have done this, but she did help to distribute some of the grace which Christ had already super-abundantly acquired.

Therefore, in the case of subjective redemption, "coredemptrix" is a term that applies not only to the Blessed Mother but rather to any woman who has helped to distribute redemptive grace. For this reason, the proper question to ask is not whether Mary is a coredemptrix, but rather in what particular sense does the term apply to her above all others?

The answer to this question is found in the definition of objective redemption. For many women can be said to have participated in subjective redemption, in releasing redemptive grace, but only Mary has a claim to have participated in objective redemption, in the acquisition of redemptive grace, as well.

At this point it should be again stated that the super-abundance of redemptive grace which is now available to us all was acquired by the Son of God, Jesus Christ, being offered on the Cross at Calvary. His sacrificial death on the Cross acquired, once for all, the super-abundance of redemptive grace which has now made redemption possible for us all.

However, and exactly because of this fact, if it can be established that Mary's participation was required in order for the redemptive offering of Christ on the Cross at Calvary to be made then her role as Coredemptrix will be confirmed. I hold that Sacred Scripture, Sacred Tradition, and the Magisterium of the Catholic Church will show that Mary participated in the offering of Christ at Calvary in two critical and indispensable ways. Ways so indispensable that it can be properly said that without the cooperation of Mary, Christ's offering on the Cross of his "flesh for the life of the world" (John 6:51) at Calvary could not have taken place.

Mary's role as Coredemptrix can only truly be understood with regard to Christ's sacrificial offering at Calvary. Yet in order to understand Calvary more fully we must ask ourselves some questions about the event.

The first premise that must be established is that Calvary was a sacrifice. The Book of Hebrews speaks of Christ as being the one sacrifice that has made all of the former sacrifices made under the old covenant no longer necessary.

> For this reason, when he came into the world, he said: Sacrifice and offering you did not desire, but a body you prepared for me; holocausts and sin offerings you took no delight in. Then I said, 'As is written of me in the scroll, Behold, I come to do your will, O God' (Hebrews 10:5-7).

In explaining this passage, the author of Hebrews states:

> He takes away the first to establish the second. By this will,' we have been consecrated through the offering of the body of Jesus Christ once for all (Hebrews 10:10).

Therefore, in this passage we not only see that Calvary was a sacrifice, but we also see that what was sacrificed at Calvary was "the body of Jesus Christ once for all."

Since we now know that Calvary was a sacrifice, and what was sacrificed at Calvary, the next logical question to ask is "Who provided the offering?" Since the offering was "the body of Jesus Christ once for all" we must now return to the moment of the incarnation (the making into flesh) of God into man in order to gain a better insight into the redemptive act of Calvary. In doing so the Annunciation (Luke 1:26-38) begins to come into focus as being a critical moment in salvation history.

Saint Bernard of Clairvaux felt that the Annunciation was such a critical moment that he describes the scene as:

> "The whole world on bended knees" awaiting Mary's response to the angel, for on it will depend in a word "the salvation of all the children of Adam, of your whole race."1

In order to understand why this was such a critical moment one must be reminded that Christ offered his "flesh for the life of the world" (John 6:51) at Calvary. Yet, logically speaking, in order for Christ to have flesh to offer Christ had to become incarnate—God had to become man.

And it was only through the freely given fiat, or yes, of Mary to God's plan, as announced by the angel Gabriel at the Annunciation, that this was able to take place. Her free consent to God's plan thus led directly to the redemption of all creation.

Without the fiat, or yes, of Mary at the Annunciation the offering of Christ simply could not have taken place. And we have no guarantee that God would have found another channel for human redemption had Mary said "no" at the Annunciation.

Catholic theology rejects voluntarism and insists that God does not act in arbitrary ways but must always act according to the divine character. For this reason, God requires the free cooperation of the human person. For to force or compel humans to follow Him violates God's very own nature. In this case, Mary, representing all of mankind, had to freely give her fiat, or yes, at the Annunciation in order for God's plan for the redemption for all mankind and creation to take place.

Therefore, because of her fiat, or yes, at the Annunciation Mary helped to acquire, in an instrumental sense, the flesh of Christ. And this very flesh of Christ is what was offered at Calvary for the redemption of all creation. For this reason, and this reason alone, it is proper to call Mary the Coredemptrix, along with her Son and our Redeemer Jesus Christ, of all mankind and creation.

Yet our Blessed Mother's role as Coredemptrix does not end at the Annunciation. As the Prophet Simeon shows, Mary is inseparably bound to the sufferings of her son.

> Behold, this child is destined for the fall and rise of many in Israel, and to be a sign that will be contradicted (and you yourself a sword will pierce) so that the thoughts of many hearts may be revealed (Luke 2:34-35).

In his Encyclical Letter "Mother of the Redeemer" Pope John Paul II said of this passage:

> Simeon's words seem like a second Annunciation to Mary, for they tell her

> of the actual historical situation in which the Son is to accomplish his mission, namely, in misunderstanding and sorrow. While this announcement on the one hand confirms her faith in the accomplishment of the divine promises of salvation, on the other hand it also reveals to her that she will have to live her obedience of faith in suffering, at the side of the suffering Savior, and her motherhood will be mysterious and sorrowful.2

So, with the rights and honors of Mary's motherhood will also come great suffering.

The climax of Mary's role as Coredemptrix comes at Calvary. This can only be the case because Mary's role as Coredemptrix takes place only in the shadow of her son Jesus Christ's role as the Redeemer of all mankind and creation. Therefore, because Christ's role comes to a climax at Calvary so must Mary's. Now in returning to our discussion about

Calvary let us review what we have learned so far about the event.

First, we established that Calvary was a sacrifice. The object of sacrifice at Calvary was "the body of Jesus Christ once for all." Ultimately, God provided the sacrifice, however the free cooperation of the Blessed Virgin Mary was necessary, in an instrumental sense, as well. This free cooperation of Mary took place initially at the Annunciation but did not end there. So, we now know there was a sacrifice, and we know who provided the sacrifice. Therefore, the next logical step we need to take is to determine who offered the sacrifice at Calvary?

The first difficulty encountered in attempting to answer this question is that the role of priest (the one who offers sacrifice) at Calvary may not be an exclusive one. Perhaps a helpful analogy in understanding this would be to remember that the sacrifice of the Mass is intimately connected to Calvary. Now we know that at the Mass one ordained priest is the primary person who offers the sacrifice. However, we also know that the lay people contribute to the offertory and are called in general to an active participation at Mass.

In establishing who served as the primary priest at Calvary the Book of Hebrews is of immense help.

> But when Christ came as high priest of the good things that have come to be, passing through the greater and more perfect tabernacle not made by hands, that is, not belonging to this creation, he entered once for all the sanctuary, not with the blood of goats and calves but with his own blood, thus obtaining eternal redemption (Hebrews 9:11-12).

The Book of Hebrews thus unmasks the great irony of Calvary. That the victim who was offered also served as the "high priest."

Yet Jesus does not offer himself alone on

Calvary. For his mother Mary, as she had already done at the Presentation, once again offers her son. As the "Dogmatic Constitution on the Church" of the Second Vatican Council states:

> Thus the Blessed Virgin advanced in her pilgrimage of faith, and faithfully persevering in her union with her Son onto the Cross, where she stood, in keeping with the divine plan, enduring with her only begotten Son the intensity of his suffering, associated herself with his sacrifice in her mother's heart, and lovingly consented to the immolation of this victim which was born of her.3

Mary follows her Son to the Cross and also endures "the intensity of his suffering." And, even beyond all of this, she consents to the immolation, the crushing, of the victim. Yet this begs the question: Why would Mary need to give her consent to Calvary?

The answer to this question is found in the Marian writings of Pope Benedict XV.

> Pope Benedict XV (1914-1922) not only confirms the doctrine of Mary's Coredemption as taught by the modern popes but articulates this Marian truth with even greater clarity. "...The fact that she was with her Son crucified and dying, was in accord with the divine plan. To such an extent did she [Mary] suffer and almost die with her suffering and dying Son; to such an extent did she surrender her maternal rights over her Son for man's salvation, and immolated Him - insofar as she could - in order to appease the justice of God, that we may rightly say she redeemed the human race together with Christ."[4]

All mothers have a right to nourish, protect, and defend the lives of their children. This is a right of nature, and in Mary's case, a right of grace. So if Mary had insisted to God that

Christ not be harmed there are good reasons to think that God would have obliged. However, she did not. Therefore, we can say that Mary consented to the offering of her Son at Calvary and thus, in a secondary and subordinate way, participated in the offering of the sacrifice.

This consent to Christ's suffering at Calvary, and her own position as His mother, led Mary into a deep participation in her Son's sufferings. Pope John Paul II says of it:

> It was on Calvary that Mary's suffering, besides the suffering of Jesus, reached an intensity which can hardly be imagined from a human point of view but which was mysteriously and supernaturally fruitful for the Redemption of the world. Her ascent of Calvary and her standing at the foot of the cross together with the beloved disciple were a special sort of sharing in the redeeming death of her Son.5

In light of this "special sort of sharing" by Mary in Christ's redemptive death on the cross at Calvary it is safe to say that Mary participated in a special way in the offering of the sacrifice of her Son.

Mary can therefore be said to have provided, in an instrumental sense, the object of the sacrifice, the body of Christ, at Calvary. Further, she can be said to have, in a secondary and subordinate sense, helped to offer the sacrifice at Calvary. These two facts, and these two facts alone, can be said to have established that Mary is the Coredemptrix of all mankind and creation! And that we can be safe to in saying, along with the Early Fathers, "Death through Eve, life through Mary."6

Yet just what are the implications to the faithful in the greater proclamation of Mary's role as Coredemptrix? In closing, allow me to offer the thought of Reverend Arthur Burton Calkins.

> While Mary's role as Coredemptrix is unique because of her unique relationship to Christ, she is nonetheless the perfect human prototype of collaborating in the work of salvation and sharing in the sufferings of Christ for the sake of his body the Church (Col. 1:24). She is, in the words of Pope John Paul II "the highest model of cooperation in the work of salvation." Hence not only does the consideration of her coredemptive role elucidate her greatness and title to the highest honor that may be given to a human being (hyperdulia), but it also illuminates the role and call of all Christians.7

Therefore, we see at work again the theological axiom that what is true of Mary should be true, to a lesser extent, of us.

Mary Coredemptrix is indeed a model for every follower of Christ. Thus, the truth about her role being proclaimed can only promote, and not hinder, Christian unity. The objective redemption brought about by Christ's offering at Calvary leads directly to our ability to participate in the subjective redemption which is at the very heart and mission of the Church.

In this way we are shown a great truth of the spiritual life: That the subjective can, and often does, cooperate with the objective. That we, as mere human beings in all of our subjectivity, can find and release God's power in the form of the super-abundance of grace that Christ has acquired not just for us many, but for us all!

References

1. O'Carrol, M., Theotokos: A Theological Encyclopedia of the Blessed Virgin Mary. Collegeville, MI: Liturgical Press, 1982, p. 106-107.

2. See section 16 of the encyclical letter of John Paul II, Mother of the Redeemer. Boston: Pauline Books, 1987.

3. See number 58 of the Vatican II document, Dogmatic Constitution on the Church.

4. Miravalle, M., Mary: Coredemptrix, Mediatrix, Advocate. Santa Barbara, CA: Queenship Publishing, 1993, p. 16-17.

5. See section 25 of the apostolic letter of John Paul II Salvifici Dolorus. Boston: Pauline Books, 1984.

6. Documents of Vatican II Dogmatic Constitution on the Church. N. 56.

7. Calkins, A., Mary: Coredemptrix, Mediatrix, Advocate: Theological Foundations II. Ed. M. Miravalle. Santa Barbara, CA: Queenship Publishing, 1996, p. 145-146.

All Biblical quotations taken from The New American Bible.

***

***

***

ABOUT THE AUTHOR

John C. Wilhelmsson is an author and professor of philosophy at San Jose State University. He founded "Chaos To Order Publishing" in 2012.

Its first release was his bestselling book of original philosophical research The Transposition of Edith Stein: Her Contributions to Philosophy, Feminism, and The Theology of the Body. This was followed up by the true story of A Pilgrimage to Iceland.

Currently, plans are in the works to revive, in a new English translation with new illustrations, the works of the great Icelandic writer and Jesuit priest Jon Sveinsson (Nonni).

You can learn more at the Chaos To Order Publishing website (www.c2op.com).

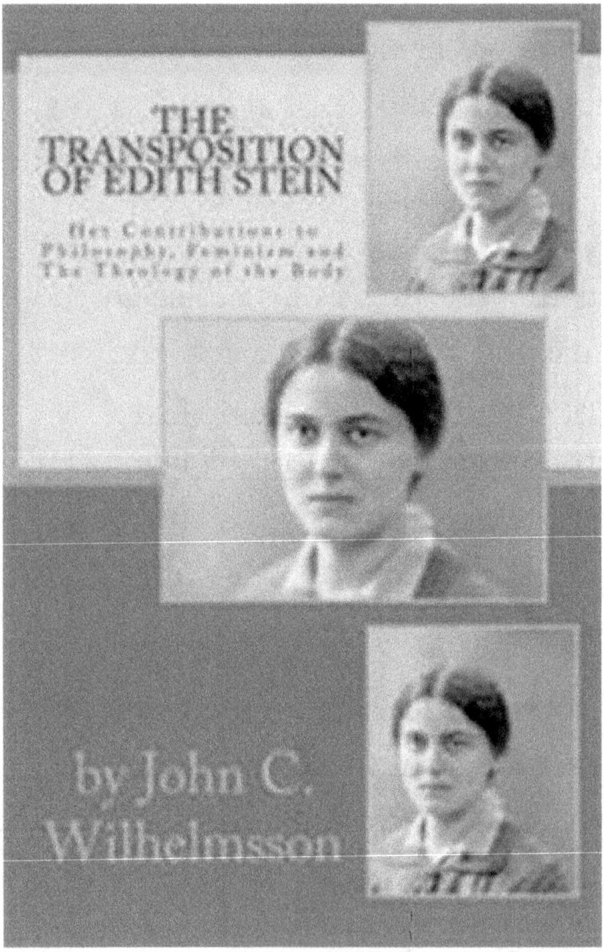
THE
TRANSPOSITION
OF EDITH STEIN
by John C.
Wilhelmsson

Before she was a saint she was a fine philosopher yet because she was a woman her contributions were ignored. This book asks the question: "Did Edith Stein make any important contributions to philosophy and, if so, what are the implications of them for us today?" It begins with a biography of Stein up until the acceptance of her doctoral dissertation "On the Problem of Empathy" in 1916. It then examines the phenomenology of Stein and, in new research, demonstrates her contributions to 20th century philosophy as a whole. Finally, it looks at the feminist thought of Stein and its direct connection to "The Theology of the Body" of Pope John Paul II. Based upon an award winning thesis, here is a book that finally goes beyond just looking at Stein's thought as a curiosity and instead makes a strong argument for her contributions to philosophy, feminism, and "The Theology of the Body."

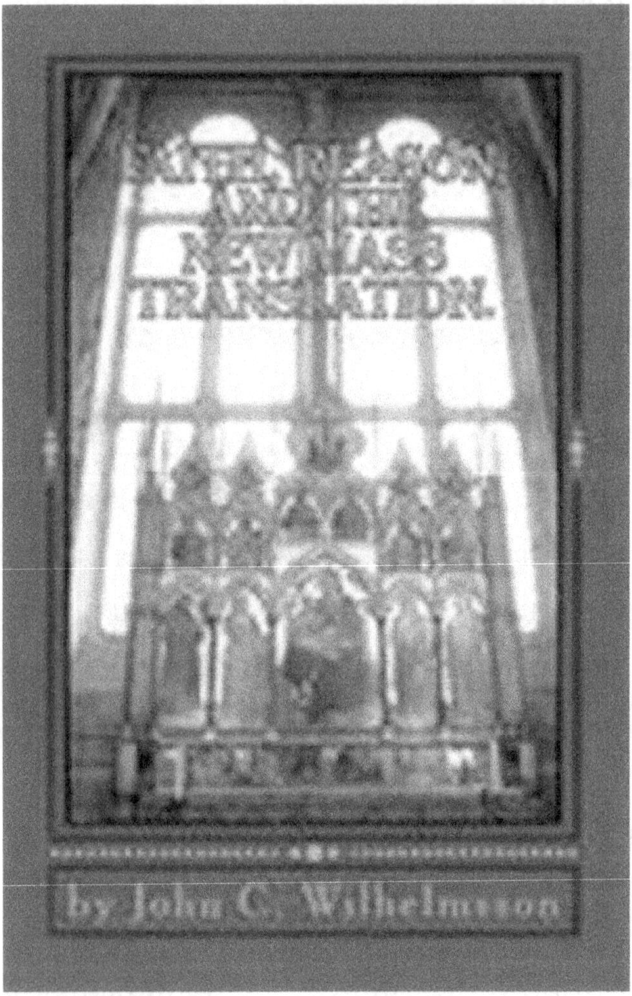
by John C. Wilhelmsson

In late 2011 the Catholic Mass was changed from the clear modern English of the Novus Ordo Mass to an obtuse literal translation from the Latin. According to the Catholic theological principle "Lex Orandi, Lex Credendi" this change in the prayer of the Church also brought with it a change in the belief of the Church. This book details the translation change and the effect it is having on Catholic belief. It also delves into the history of the issue and what the agenda behind the change actually was. Featuring, "The Old 'We Believe' Crowd," "A Tale of Two Traditions," and the basic ordinary text of the 1973 Novus Ordo Mass, here is a reflection on the Mass that has shaped the faith of the English speaking Catholic world for the past 40 years, along with an argument why its demise was unjust even according to the principles of Catholic thought itself.

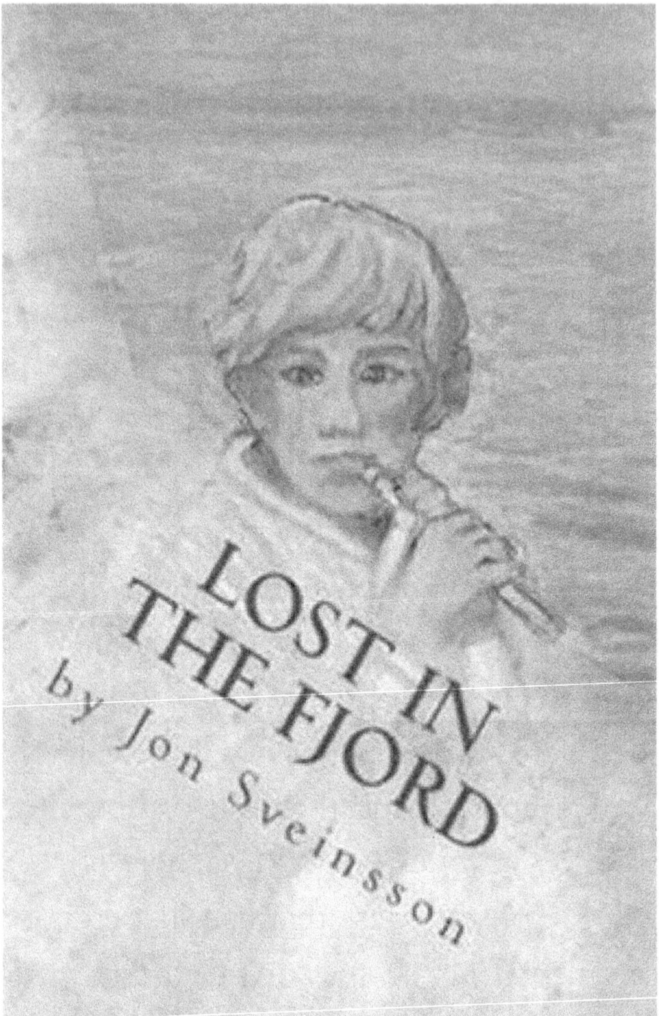
LOST IN
THE FJORD
by Jon Sveinsson

Nonni and his younger brother Manni are Icelandic boys who live in the charming town of Akureyri. Nonni is curious about many things yet forgetful of his parents' warnings, while Manni is pure of heart and loyal toward Nonni. Thinking he can lure the fish out of the sea with his magic flute, Nonni, with Manni at his side, sets out upon the great Eyjafjörður Fjord in a row boat to try. Great adventures follow in this classic and true story of virtue and vocation!

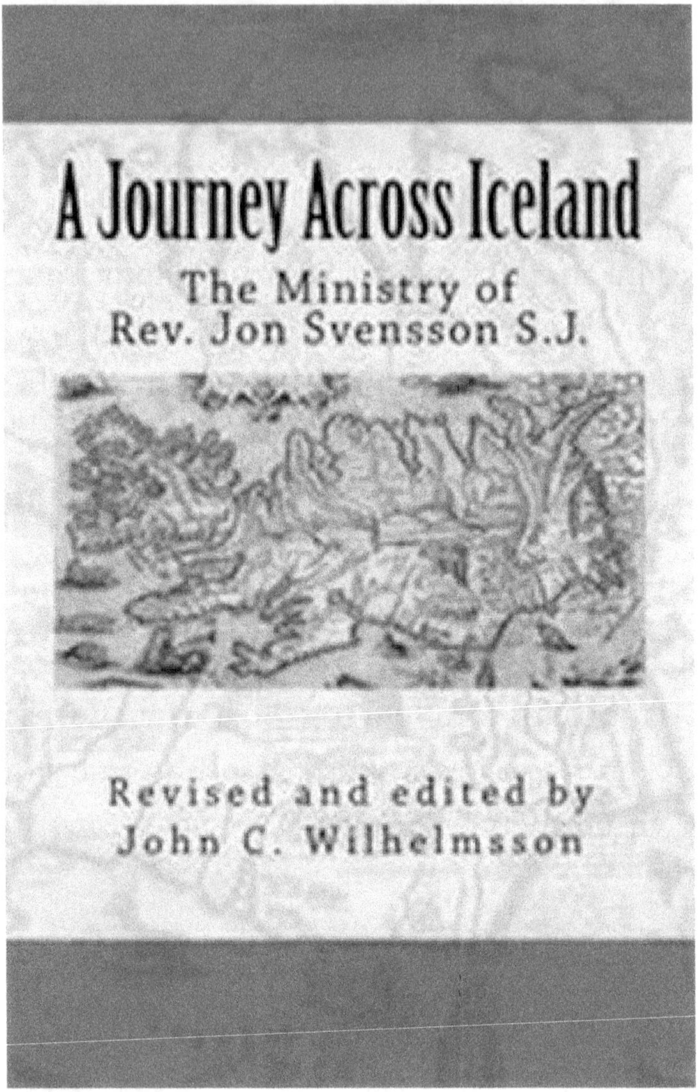
A Journey Across Iceland
The Ministry of
Rev. Jon Svensson S.J.
Revised and edited by
John C. Wilhelmsson

Jon Sveinsson (or "Nonni") is the only Jesuit priest ever born in Iceland. He left his homeland as a boy, with his beloved brother Armann (or "Manni"), to follow their mutual call to become Jesuit missionaries. Although Manni has since passed on during his studies, Nonni is now the Reverend Jon Sveinsson. The boys had wished to become Jesuit missionaries, like St. Francis Xavier, yet Jon Sveinsson has spent most of his time in the order so far as either a student or instructor in academia. Still longing to fulfill his dream of becoming a missionary he has volunteered to travel to Iceland to care for the souls of his fellow countrymen. And now, after some amount of time, that call is about to be received. Such is the premise of this classic Icelandic travelogue written by the man who would later become one of the most beloved children's authors of all time.

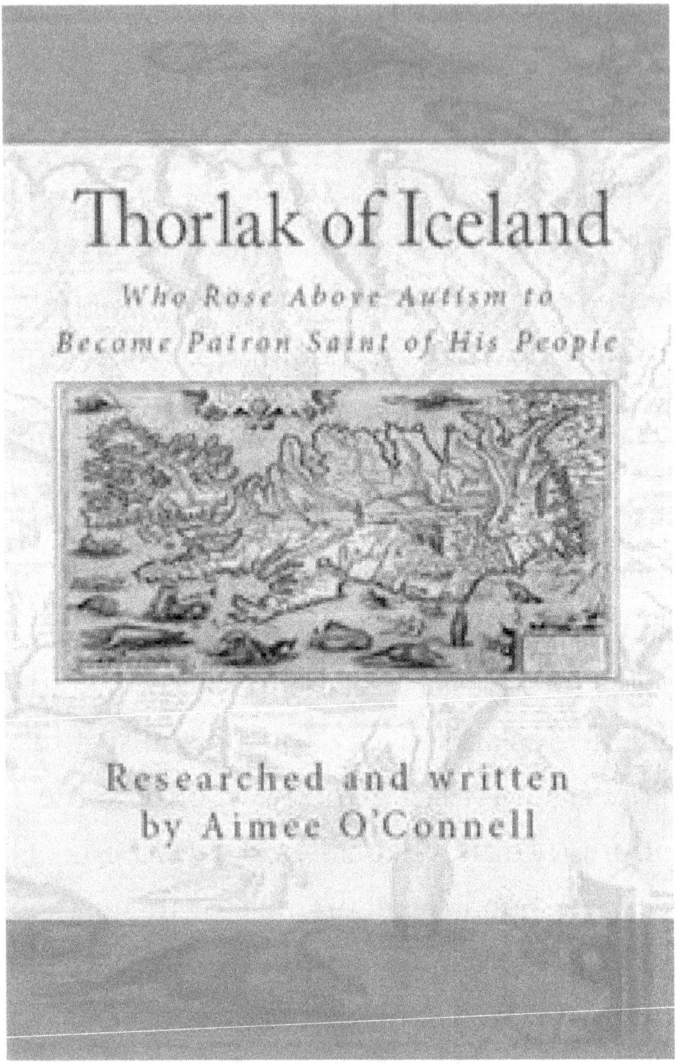
Thorlak of Iceland
Who Rose Above Autism to
Become Patron Saint of His People
Researched and written
by Aimee O'Connell

Iceland's history is told in the stories of its celebrated figures. From Viking explorers to Saga heroes, the voices that define Icelandic culture are well known. Yet one man in Iceland's past had difficulty finding the words to form his own voice and be known for who he really was: Thorlák Thórhallsson, declared by his people "The Patron Saint of Iceland" in 1198 and officially canonized by Pope John Paul II in 1984. Yet, despite these honors, few have ever heard Thorlák's complete and true story: A child prodigy treated as an adult by those around him, a sorrowful boy from a broken home, a scholar of the emerging theology of merciful love, an innovator in pastoral leadership, and a man who understood the fundamental need to love and be loved. Thorlák of Iceland is an opportunity at last to celebrate this quiet hero who embodies the spiritual heart of the Icelandic people, and to learn from his inspiring true story wisdom for our own age.

www.ingramcontent.com/pod-product-compliance
Lightning Source LLC
LaVergne TN
LVHW021504080426
835509LV00018B/2396
* 9 7 8 0 9 8 8 6 5 6 3 4 5 *